CW01085841

PICTURE OURSELVES IN LATVIA

BY **ROSS HOWARD**

SERVING THEATRE

SINCE 1830

SAMUELFRENCH-LONDON.CO.UK
SAMUELFRENCH.COM

FOR AMATEUR PRODUCTION ENQUIRIES

UNITED KINGDOM AND WORLD EXCLUDING NORTH AMERICA

plays@SamuelFrench-London.co.uk

020 7255 4302/01

Each title is subject to availability from Samuel French,

depending upon country of performance.

MUSIC USE NOTE

Licensees are solely responsible for obtaining formal written permission from copyright owners to use copyrighted music in the performance of this play and are strongly cautioned to do so. If no such permission is obtained by the licensee, then the licensee must use only original music that the licensee owns and controls. Licensees are solely responsible and liable for all music clearances and shall indemnify the copyright owners of the play(s) and their licensing agent, Samuel French, against any costs, expenses, losses and liabilities arising from the use of music by licensees. Please contact the appropriate music licensing authority in your territory for the rights to any incidental music.

IMPORTANT BILLING AND CREDIT REQUIREMENTS

If you have obtained performance rights to this title, please refer to your licensing agreement for important billing and credit requirements.

Picture Ourselves in Latvia was first produced by New Light Theater Project at Access Theater, New York City on July 10 2014. Directed by Sarah Norris. The cast was as follows:

DR RUPERT – **Christian Ryan**

NURSE WHITEHALL – **Amy Lee Pearsall**

OLIVER – **Gregory James Cohan**

MARTIN – **Christopher Daftsios**

DUNCAN – **Andy Nogasky**

ANNA – **Dana Benningfield**

Set Design	**Oliver Sohngen**
Costume Design	**Samantha Lind**
Lighting Design	**Michael O'Connor**
Sound Design Production	**Kyle C. Norris**
Stage Management	**Juni Li**
Associate Director	**Abby Wylan**
Assistant Director/ASM	**Nick Walsh**
ASM/Technical Assistant	**Scott Pulvirent**
Casting Director	**Alex Lawrence**
Producer	**Michael Aguirre**

For Jerry L. Crawford

Acknowledgements : Hannah Pierce, Euan Borland,
Timothy Trimingham Lee, Minna Pang, Stephen Kelly,
Duncan Wilkinson, Adam Welsh, Duncan Pearse, Jessica Jordan-
Wrench, Nick DiCola, Kat Heath, Quinn Corbin, Mike Aguirre,
Amanda Berry, Lauren Schaefer, Ron Lasko, Eleanor Rhode,
Jamie Richards, Antonia Reid, Samuel John, Neil McPherson
and all at Finborough Theatre, Adam Thorpe, Mary Doherty,
Mark Donald, Gemma Lawrence, Nathan Nolan,
Aled Pedrick and Matthew Raymond.

Picture Ourselves in Latvia

by Ross Howard

CHARACTERS

DR. RUPERT – A psychiatrist. Very English.

NURSE WHITEHALL – A nurse.

OLIVER – An orderly.

MARTIN – A patient.

DUNCAN – A patient.

ANNA – A patient. Very Latvian.

PLACE & NOTES

With the exception of Scene 6, the play takes place on a psychiatric ward in England.

A dash (–) after a word denotes an interruption or an inability to complete the word or sentence. An ellipsis (…) denotes a trailing off.

A loose translation of the Latvian folk song *ES IZJĀJU PRŪŠU ZEMI* as sung in Scene 4 is as follows :

"I RODE OFF TO THE LAND OF PRUSSIANS
WHILE PLAYING THE ZITHER.
PRUSSIAN GIRLS WANTED
TO HAVE ME AS THEIR OWN SIR
I WON'T STAY WITH THE PRUSSIAN GIRLS
I'VE GOT MYSELF ONE IN KURZEME
IN KURZEME THERE ALREADY IS ONE FOR MYSELF
A YOUNG MAIDEN IN MY YARD
MAY GOD BE WITH YOU, PRUSSIAN GIRLS.
I AM GOING BACK TO KURZEME
BACK TO KURZEME. BACK TO MY OWN GIRL."

Scene One

OLIVER, **MARTIN** *and* **ANNA** *are doing press ups.*

OLIVER Forty eight… forty nine… fifty.

OLIVER jumps to his feet. He is full of energy. **MARTIN** *and* **ANNA** *look exhausted and get to their feet in a weary manner.*

Not so easy, is it? Now imagine doing nine hundred of those in four minutes. That's what we had to do out there. On the deck.

MARTIN Wow, nine hundred?

OLIVER Nine hundred, Martin. The big nine-oh-oh. Two fat ladies.

ANNA Two fat ladies?

OLIVER Tell her, Martin.

MARTIN It's a bingo reference, Anna. We say it after every number, don't we, Oliver?

OLIVER We do indeed, Martini Extra Dry. It's a British tradition.

ANNA Two fat ladies, eighty-eight.

MARTIN Yes, that's it. Sort of.

OLIVER Yeah, other way round but you're half way there. Now imagine doing all nine hundred when you're feeling sea sick.

MARTIN I couldn't. Could you, Anna? I couldn't.

OLIVER You probably couldn't, Martin. But see, that's where I come in, see. And the people like me. Because me and the rest of our boys could; and that's how we do what we do and how we did what we did for you. You get me?

MARTIN Er, I think so.

OLIVER I mean some people call us heroes but I wouldn't know about that. Well, I do know about that but I wouldn't like to say.

Brief silence.

So... ?

MARTIN What?

OLIVER I mean, well like, do you think I'm a, that I'm well, like a hero, Martin?

MARTIN Oh I wouldn't like to say really.

OLIVER Don't be shy now.

No response.

Anna?

ANNA *shrugs her shoulders.*

You're too shy with your feelings you two. That's your trouble. Probably why you're in here. Mad with shyness. Hey, you want to hear a story? They say it's the greatest story ever told.

MARTIN Is this about Jesus?

OLIVER No. Well, that probably is the greatest story ever told. *(A beat)* No, actually I reckon this one and that one are neck and neck.

MARTIN Six of one and half a dozen of the other.

OLIVER Exactly. Too close to call. But it's a fucking belter, it's about the day I sank The Belgrano.

DUNCAN *enters.*

MARTIN Duncan!

OLIVER Dunconi.

DUNCAN Martin. *(To* **OLIVER***)* Bullshitting again? You big bullshitter.

MARTIN Oliver was going to tell us a story. Weren't you, Oliver?

DUNCAN I bet he was.

MARTIN The greatest story ever told. Joint first place.

DUNCAN The biggest bullshit ever told and runaway winner more like.

OLIVER Eh. Now, now. Don't get cheeky.

Silence.

DUNCAN I actually wanted to ask Anna something. Anna, do you have a second?

ANNA *looks over to* **DUNCAN** *but does not move.*

OLIVER Fire away, Dunc.

DUNCAN *(To* **ANNA***)* In private.

ANNA *does not move.*

OLIVER No secrets in here, big boy.

DUNCAN Anna?

OLIVER She doesn't want to go with you. Say what you've got to say here. We won't laugh will we, Martin?

MARTIN I don't know what he's going to say yet. He might say something funny.

OLIVER He might.

MARTIN Duncan can make me laugh, can't you Duncan?

DUNCAN Yes, Martin.

Silence.

Anna. I was thinking about watching a film in the common area. Would you like to watch it with me?

OLIVER He's asking you out on a date, Anna.

DUNCAN NO IT'S NOT!

OLIVER *laughs.*

ANNA Can Martin come to? Do you want to watch a film, Martin?

DUNCAN Well, I was just asking you.

MARTIN I want to hear the story.

ANNA I want to hear the story too.

OLIVER It's better than a film.

Silence.

MARTIN Stay and listen to the story, Duncan. Then maybe you and Anna can watch the film.

ANNA I don't want to if you can't.

MARTIN If you don't want me to watch the film with you, Duncan, I can go to my room and go to sleep or do some other stuff.

Pause.

DUNCAN Go on then. What's this story?

OLIVER Oh, I don't think this story is for you, Dunconi.

DUNCAN Why's that?

MARTIN He hates it when you call him 'Dunconi', doesn't he, Anna?

    ANNA *nods.*

DUNCAN So why's it not a story for me?

OLIVER Has water in it.

DUNCAN So?

OLIVER Don't like water, do you? You're scared of water aren't you, Duncan?

DUNCAN I'm not scared of water.

OLIVER Just the thought of it makes you lose your shit.

DUNCAN No *(A beat)* just don't like showers. Being splashed.

OLIVER And that's why you stink. Anna doesn't want to sit next to that. She wouldn't be able to taste her popcorn.

DUNCAN I don't have popcorn. And I don't stink. I have baths.

OLIVER Shallow baths. Like a baby.

DUNCAN They're still baths. Gets the job done.

OLIVER Pussy.

    DR. RUPERT *enters.*

DR. RUPERT Good afternoon, ladies and gentleman.

OLIVER Doctor.

DR. RUPERT *(To* **OLIVER***)* Everything hunky dory?

OLIVER Sound as a pound.

DR. RUPERT Good. Now are we all looking forward to Nurse Whitehall coming back?

No response.

Well of course, none of you have ever met her so that's understandable. I think you'll like her. She's very nice. Good.

MARTIN She's had a little baby.

DR. RUPERT That's right, Martin.

MARTIN Will she bring it with her, do you think, Doctor? So we can all have a look?

DR. RUPERT *(Laughs)* Oh well, I'm not sure about that.

MARTIN They do that, don't they? Mothers. At the workplace.

DR. RUPERT Probably. Yes, I think they do. But we are a psychiatric ward. It just depends.

MARTIN I bet it has baths like you, Duncan. Shallow baths so it doesn't drown.

DR. RUPERT Well, you all sound in good spirits. Just wanted to pop my head in and say *bonjour*.

MARTIN Oliver is going to tell us a story.

DR. RUPERT How exciting. Another time for me, I'm afraid. Anna, Duncan. *(A beat) Arrivederci.*

  DR. RUPERT *exits.*

MARTIN That's Italian for goodbye.

  Silence.

OLIVER *(To* **DUNCAN***)* Go and watch television.

DUNCAN No, I want to stay.

  Silence.

OLIVER Okay, so we're in the South Atlantic. Stormy weather, choppy waters. Sharks, killer whales, dolphins, sea dragons, you name it. They have everything down there. Jumping up, rocking the ship, we're shaking from side to side, we're losing men right and left. We're all soaked. Thousands of gallons spraying up, we were submerged, you know.

DUNCAN I'm going to watch television.

OLIVER Oh no, stay.

MARTIN I think he wants to go.

DUNCAN Anna?

No response. Silence.

I'm going to watch television. *(A beat)* There's no such thing as Sea Dragons.

> **DUNCAN** *exits.*

OLIVER Ha! He wouldn't know. He wasn't there. I don't think he'd have had the stomach for it anyway. Good job he wasn't there. We'd have lost the war.

MARTIN What war?

OLIVER This was the Falklands, Martin. England versus Argentina. I'm telling the story. The Brazilians were thinking of getting involved too, I think. Chickened out probably. Plus this was 1982, they had a World Cup in Spain to light up.

MARTIN How old were you?

OLIVER How long's a piece a string, Martin? Besides, don't be so rude.

MARTIN I'm sorry, Oliver.

OLIVER In a word, the war is going really badly for us. Margaret Thatcher calls us up on Skype and says as much. We had Skype back then. The Navy gets all kind of things way before you civvies get them. She asks for me personally. I guess she heard through the grapevine about my bravery over there in Gibraltar.

ANNA What did you do in Gibraltar?

OLIVER Oh that gets you excited, Anna? That's another story for another time. So Prime Minister Thatcher is there with the Queen and some other famous people from the entertainment industry. Sean Connery, maybe Tom Jones, I don't know. I was more focused on the mission than getting anyone to send autographs. Anyway, she says there's an Argentine ship very close to us and it's called The Belgrano.

MARTIN That's a good name for a ship. Very exotic.

OLIVER Yeah, pretty exotic. They were exotic climes that we were in, Martin. All kinds of names like that were involved. Rio Grande, Tierra del Fuego, Goose Green. You name it. Anyway, she says "Oliver, if you see it, sink it." Then she adds "For me" and then we lose the connection. Then, have a guess what happened next?

MARTIN You sank it?

OLIVER You're jumping the gun, Martin. I had to see it first, mate.

MARTIN So when did you see it?

OLIVER Well, that's what happened next. Out of the corner of my eye, I see it. And it's coming towards us. Or moving away from us. It's there anyway.

MARTIN And you knew that was it?

OLIVER It had to be. It says The Belgrano on it. And it's got all these grinning Argies shouting "*Ariba! Ariba!*" on it and they're holding machine guns. So that's when I reached for my bazooka.

MARTIN Wow. A bazooka.

OLIVER Took me two shots. Boom boom. Sunk the bastard. All you could hear was the sound of squealing Argies falling into the sea covered in flames. It changed everything that moment. Prime Minister Thatcher wouldn't have won the next general election if that hadn't happened. We wouldn't be where are today if I hadn't done that. I mean, we'd all be speaking Spanish for one thing.

MARTIN Good for you. Hey, Anna?

ANNA Yes, good for you.

OLIVER Thanks, guys. It was my finest hour. It was our finest hour when I sunk that bastard.

Scene Two

NURSE WHITEHALL *is eating her lunch and engrossed in a book.* **OLIVER** *is slumped in a chair half playing with his phone and half watching* **DUNCAN** *and* **MARTIN** *who arm wrestle repeatedly nearby.* **MARTIN** *does not seem to put up any resistance to* **DUNCAN** *who keeps winning easily/instantly.* **DUNCAN** *is beginning to find this tiresome while* **MARTIN** *seems to be enjoying himself anyway.*

MARTIN You keep winning! Nurse Whitehall, Duncan keeps winning!

NURSE WHITEHALL Very good, Martin. That's very good.

MARTIN Well I keep losing. I can't work it out!

NURSE WHITEHALL Oh dear. Well perhaps that's all you deserve.

A sudden stillness and silence, which **NURSE WHITEHALL** *notices.*

Duncan, can you not let him play on the same team? That's what I meant.

DUNCAN It's arm wrestling.

NURSE WHITEHALL Ah.

> **NURSE WHITEHALL** *goes back to her book. Silence.* **DR. RUPERT** *enters and sees* **NURSE WHITEHALL** *for the first time in nearly a year.*

DR. RUPERT *(Awkwardly to* **NURSE WHITEHALL***)* Beep, beep.

> *No response as* **NURSE WHITEHALL** *and everyone continue what they are doing.*

> *Again, awkwardly to* **NURSE WHITEHALL**

> Bzzzzzzzzzzzzzzzzzz.

> *Again, no response as* **NURSE WHITEHALL** *and everyone continue what they are doing.* **DR. RUPERT** *weighs up trying for a third time or just leaving; or maybe even leaving and coming back and trying for a third time.* **NURSE WHITEHALL** *looks up and sees* **DR. RUPERT**.

NURSE WHITEHALL *(Suddenly)* Doctor.

DR. RUPERT *(Startled)* Nurse.

NURSE WHITEHALL Hello.

DR. RUPERT Nurse Whitehall. Ha. I didn't see you there. You blend right into that chair.

NURSE WHITEHALL I was just having lunch and reading a book.

DR. RUPERT I see. Taking in words and ideas and plot twists while taking in nutrients. Very good. Great combo. Multi-tasking. How female. *(Stops himself)* Hmmh. Yes. *(A beat)* Oliver?

OLIVER Yes, Doctor?

DR. RUPERT Common area, maybe? There's a soldier.

OLIVER Come on chaps.

> OLIVER *rounds up* **MARTIN** *and* **DUNCAN** *and they exit.*

DR.RUPERT. Oh well this is a surprise. I was just on my way to the hairdressers.

NURSE WHITEHALL Oh?

DR. RUPERT Yes. I want my hair cut.

NURSE WHITEHALL Well that sounds like a good plan going there.

DR. RUPERT Yes. It's my *modus operandi.* Ha. *(A beat)* So *Quelle surprise* indeed. What a surprise. You being here at this time.

NURSE WHITEHALL Yes. *(A beat)* It's funny but your hair always looks the same. I never know when you have anything done to it.

DR. RUPERT Oh. Well, I… I suppose I do go for trims quite frequently.

NURSE WHITEHALL It looks nice now just how it is.

DR. RUPERT Really? I detest it when it gets like this but how wonderful of you to say. You know, I had a beard while you were away.

NURSE WHITEHALL Wow. How was that?

DR. RUPERT Just for a month. Some people said it suited me but some people say things like that, don't they?

NURSE WHITEHALL Yes.

DR. RUPERT You just have to wonder what's rattling around in the heads of the silent majority. *(A beat)* Well I just well, well I didn't expect you in until this afternoon. Just on what it says on the board out there and all that.

NURSE WHITEHALL Yes, but I woke up this morning and I felt I couldn't wait to get back and then I thought 'why wait to get back'?

DR. RUPERT Why wait indeed? No, I just didn't expect it. *(A beat)* Oh not that I've ever really expected anything from you in the past, you understand.

NURSE WHITEHALL Sorry?

DR. RUPERT Oh, by that I mean, you're not always on my mind. Expecting, guessing, thinking things about you.

NURSE WHITEHALL Oh.

DR. RUPERT Wondering where you are, what you are doing etc.

NURSE WHITEHALL Right.

DR. RUPERT I think Elizabeth would have something to say about that! *(A beat)* My wife Elizabeth, I mean.

NURSE WHITEHALL Of course.

DR. RUPERT Not you, Elizabeth. Gosh. I still marvel at that coincidence.

NURSE WHITEHALL Me too. And you a Robert.

DR. RUPERT Yes. Me, a Robert married to an Elizabeth and you an Elizabeth married to a Robert. That never gets old.

NURSE WHITEHALL What are we like?

DR. RUPERT Yes, it's a good thing we have our labels, isn't it? And our last names.

NURSE WHITEHALL Doctor Rupert.

DR. RUPERT Nurse Whitehall.

They laugh.

NURSE WHITEHALL Those little names we call each other.

DR. RUPERT Those cheeky monikers. Otherwise it could be a minefield.

NURSE WHITEHALL Yes, I think we've done well to keep it uncomplicated.

Silence.

How is Elizabeth?

DR. RUPERT Oh, you know. How's Robert? Actually, it doesn't matter really. Anyway, yes, you coming in early today. Making a mockery of the shift board behind reception. You are capable of the unexpected, Nurse Whitehall.

NURSE WHITEHALL I try my best.

DR. RUPERT You're an unpredictable Lady of the – I was going to say 'night' but that's a prostitute, isn't it? I meant, "Realm". I'm sorry. *(A beat)* Let's just say…

NURSE WHITEHALL I'm unpredictable?

DR. RUPERT Yes. A maverick.

NURSE WHITEHALL I accept the compliment.

DR. RUPERT You should. It was a compliment. I was complimenting you. I just never know what quite to expect from you!

NURSE WHITEHALL Ha!

DR. RUPERT Except when you were *expecting* yourself perhaps. See what I did there?

NURSE WHITEHALL Yes.

DR. RUPERT Yes, I expected you would have a child when you were pregnant, and you did. I knew you'd go all the way. How is she by the way? He? It?

NURSE WHITEHALL She. Charlotte's –

DR. RUPERT I've really missed you. *(A beat)* I'm sorry. Did I say that out loud? How embarrassing. As a colleague probably. We've missed you on the ward. I thought you were coming this afternoon. I needed my hair cutting anyway. It was just when they could fit me in. Yours looks great.

NURSE WHITEHALL Are you alright, Doctor?

DR. RUPERT Who? Me? Why do you ask?

NURSE WHITEHALL Yes. You seem…

DR. RUPERT I do, don't I? It feels like a mild panic attack. How strange. Let's talk later. Oh no, I think I'll stay. I'm here now. I'm fine. Yes. Spot of hay fever, I think.

NURSE WHITEHALL In winter? I didn't think you suffered from it.

DR. RUPERT I know. It's all change round here. Ha. No, they've got me on this new medication for it that I haven't started yet. They say late spring I should probably get going on it. Which makes more sense season wise. It's probably the panic attack I mentioned. It's very hot in here all of a sudden. It's so great to have you back. I'm sorry.

Silence.

Oh I think it's over now. Why don't we just get back to the basics? Work. So you've met them, then? The patients?

NURSE WHITEHALL Oh yes. They're very interesting. But then they always are, aren't they? Martin is –

DR. RUPERT So how's home life with the new arrival? Must be quite a change. Is it the strain on marriage they say it is? Getting up multiple times in the night, lack of sleep, leading to all kinds of arguments and then the tinge of regret of what you've got yourself into?

NURSE WHITEHALL Who says that? *(A beat)* Do you want to sit down?

DR. RUPERT Oh no, thank you.

NURSE WHITEHALL You've started sweating. You should sit down.

DR. RUPERT Have I? I'm fine standing.

NURSE WHITEHALL Okay, if you're sure.

DR. RUPERT I'd like to sit. Let's sit.

NURSE WHITEHALL There you go.

They sit. **NURSE WHITEHALL** *delves into her bag and produces two apples.*

DR. RUPERT You're very nurturing. You'd make a fine mother, if you're not already.

NURSE WHITEHALL Thank you. Would you like an apple?

DR. RUPERT Oh did you pick these yourself?

NURSE WHITEHALL No, I bought them from Tesco.

DR. RUPERT I'm fine, thank you. Actually, go on then. Hand it over. Very kind of you.

They both start eating their apples.

Is this a metaphor? Us eating apples, I don't know. What's your book by the way? It looks fantastic. *Worse Things Happen At Sea.* What a terrible title. What's it about?

NURSE WHITEHALL It's about some pirates working in the Bermuda Triangle. My mum likes him. I'm not convinced.

DR. RUPERT Do you have pictures of her? On your phone?

NURSE WHITEHALL My mother?

DR. RUPERT Your daughter. Whatever you said her name was. I know her name. It's Charlotte. I remember you saying just now.

NURSE WHITEHALL Yes. Do you want to see?

DR. RUPERT Do I?

NURSE WHITEHALL Do you?

DR. RUPERT I don't know. Do you want me to?

NURSE WHITEHALL Do I?

DR. RUPERT Do you?

NURSE WHITEHALL AND DR. RUPERT. Probably not.

DR. RUPERT I don't really want to.

NURSE WHITEHALL Good.

> *Silence.*

DR. RUPERT I feel better now. This has been incredibly awkward. I'm going to go for that haircut. Thanks for the apple.

NURSE WHITEHALL Oh, okay.

Scene Three

> **DR. RUPERT, NURSE WHITEHALL, MARTIN, DUNCAN** and **ANNA** *are seated together.* **OLIVER** *stands by and watches at a distance apart from the group.*

MARTIN … and she always wore flat shoes… when really, perhaps, with what else she always seemed to be wearing, you might think heels would have been more appropriate…

DR. RUPERT Yes.

MARTIN But maybe she had to walk a lot to get to where she was going, I don't know, I couldn't say for sure.

DR. RUPERT No. Interesting.

MARTIN And she was always reading Thomas Hardy, I always remember that. She went all the way to Cockfosters, must have lived there, I guess. I stayed on once all the way just to see. *(A brief silence)* But that's it. That's really the only time I remember being truly in love with a woman.

NURSE WHITEHALL And did you ever speak to her? Find out her name?

No response.

DUNCAN I think we all know by now he didn't.

NURSE WHITEHALL Duncan.

DUNCAN Didn't have the balls.

NURSE WHITEHALL Duncan.

DR. RUPERT Did you, Martin? Did you ever find out her name?

MARTIN No. No... I didn't...

DR. RUPERT I see. Well that's very good, Martin. Thank you for sharing that with us. Anyone else?

NURSE WHITEHALL What about you, Anna?

No response.

Anna?

ANNA *looks up.*

What about Latvia?

DR. RUPERT Yes, Anna. Tell us about Latvia. *(A beat)* Capital is Riga, we all know that, but what is its population size? Give us a figure so we can all picture it. Let us all for one moment picture ourselves in Latvia. Anna, how many people are we seeing around us? Let's say it's a sunny day and the whole population is outside walking.

NURSE WHITEHALL Lots of Latvian people, walking along swinging their arms gently in the way we all do.

DR. RUPERT Yes.

NURSE WHITEHALL I'm seeing one person with his arms out, he's approaching another person laughing.

DR. RUPERT He's chuckling. "I got your text message!" he says in Latvian. They embrace. They used to work together in a factory that burnt down. No one died. There's a history between them. A long time love that's unspoken, perhaps?

DUNCAN Are they gay?

DR. RUPERT No they're not gay. But yes, I suppose they can be.

NURSE WHITEHALL It's a man and a woman in my mind.

DR. RUPERT Natasha and Igor. So what is its population? Latvia? Rough figure? What are we talking about?

No response. Then a silence. **DUNCAN** *groans.*

NURSE WHITEHALL Duncan. What about you? You used to play tennis, didn't you?

DUNCAN Do we have to talk about the same things every meeting?

DR. RUPERT There's really no need to swear, Duncan.

MARTIN He didn't swear, did he?.

DR. RUPERT *(Sternly)* Martin. Or even shout. There's no need to shout.

ANNA Martin didn't shout.

DUNCAN Martin wasn't shouting.

NURSE WHITEHALL Okay, okay. Let's all agree to disagree.

DUNCAN But he didn't.

NURSE WHITEHALL Let's just all calm down, shall we?

DR. RUPERT Precisely. Everyone calm down. There's no need to get so excited before golf.

DUNCAN's, **ANNA**'s and **MARTIN**'s *demeanor brightens.*

MARTIN	ANNA	DUNCAN
We're playing golf?	I've never played golf.	I love golf.

NURSE WHITEHALL No one's playing golf.

DR. RUPERT Well I am. 2 o'clock.

NURSE WHITEHALL Dr. Rupert is playing golf.

DUNCAN Well maybe he wants somebody to carry his bag?

MARTIN Or... or I can lick my finger and hold it up, or, or pull up some grass and toss it up in the air to show him which way the wind is blowing. *(To the rest)* They do that, don't they? In golf?

DUNCAN *and* **ANNA** *nod.*

DR. RUPERT Now you know you have to stay here. Inside. Why don't you watch some television? Or read the newspapers. That footballer has been caught cheating on his wife again, hasn't he?

MARTIN But we always watch television.

ANNA Always.

NURSE WHITEHALL Yes, but we've recorded *Eastenders* for you. *The X-Factor* and *Strictly Come Dancing.* Don't you want to know who's going to win, Martin?

DUNCAN No one wins in *Eastenders.*

NURSE WHITEHALL Don't be childish, Duncan. *(A beat)* What about *Top Gear* and *Midsomer Murders*? What about Louis Theroux? They're a little odd, aren't they, Americans? The people he has on there, goodness.

DR. RUPERT Well I don't know about all of you, but I think the pretty one is going to win.

NURSE WHITEHALL Oh I think he'll win. He's very charismatic. He's an electrician.

DR. RUPERT Well if he wins it'll be a far cry from all that.

NURSE WHITEHALL *(Laughs)* Yes, I suppose it will. So who do we think will get Christmas Number One?

ANNA I want to clean the toilets here. Can I?

MARTIN Yes, I'd like to do that too.

DUNCAN Yeah, me too. Or mop the floors. Both even.

NURSE WHITEHALL They're not dirty are they?

DUNCAN Just for something to do.

DR. RUPERT We already have people who do that. *(A beat)* Did we all enjoy the Olympics? And the weather held. So that was something.

NURSE WHITEHALL I liked watching the opening ceremony.

DR. RUPERT The opening ceremony. Men and women in tracksuits, at the peak of physical fitness, holding up placards, as if to say "We're from this country and by Jove, we're going to do our level best".

NURSE WHITEHALL And all that choreography. It was very clever.

DR. RUPERT Slightly hesitant children in red and blue lycra, children of each ethnicity, waving ribbons.

NURSE WHITEHALL And just think it was right on our doorstep. *(A beat)* I like the swimming and cycling. Does anyone else like those events?

No response.

DR. RUPERT The swimming and cycling, yes. Recreational activities for most of us, but for them it's their life.

NURSE WHITEHALL You just needed to get into the spirit of it, I think.

DR. RUPERT Hurdles, javelin, the shot put... a young gymnast sprains her ankle, her stone-faced, possibly pushy parents look on. Is that it for their pride and joy? Will she get another chance in four years? Will she manage to keep the weight off? Teenagers should be allowed to be teenagers, but then who am I to say? My wife and I can't conceive. But that's a sad story. I really enjoyed the rowing, didn't you?

Silence.

NURSE WHITEHALL Well we have the boat race, don't we? It must be good practice for them.

DR. RUPERT True. We have a fantastic heritage. In the rowing especially. My leg hurts.

DR. RUPERT *flexes his leg. Silence.*

DUNCAN I think we'd all like to do something around here. A job of some kind. I think it would make us feel better about ourselves.

MARTIN Yes. Anything really. A job of some kind.

ANNA Me too. I'd like to do something. Just to clean the toilets. Or wipe the floors. I think we'd feel a lot more confident in our own skin if we had jobs.

DUNCAN Like Martin said, it can be anything really. Can we?

NURSE WHITEHALL Well, I'm not sure about that...

Pause.

But *Comic Relief* is around the corner.

DR. RUPERT *(Getting up)* Yes, maybe you can think of something silly we can all do for cash. Make a list. The wackier the better. Shouldn't be too difficult with your imaginations.

NURSE WHITEHALL Or maybe it's *Sport Relief*?

DR. RUPERT Ah, even better. Anyway, good session. I think we're making real progress here.

A beat.

DUNCAN We're being serious.

No response.

MARTIN And besides... I... I don't think any of us would like to imagine we'd be, where we are now... erm... then. Next year, I mean.

Silence. **DR. RUPERT** *and* **NURSE WHITEHALL** *glance at each other.*

DUNCAN We need to work. We miss it.

DR. RUPERT *and* **NURSE WHITEHALL** *glance at each other once more.*

Scene Four

MARTIN *and* **ANNA** *are seated.* **DUNCAN** *lays face down on the floor a few yards in front of them. He shows no sign of movement.* **MARTIN** *and* **ANNA** *just look at him for a few moments in silence.*

MARTIN Duncan.

No response.

Duncan.

No response.

ANNA Duncan.

No response.

Duncan.

MARTIN Duncan.

ANNA Duncan.

MARTIN Duncan.

No response.

MARTIN AND ANNA. Duncan.

No response. **MARTIN** *and* **ANNA** *continue to sit in silence.*

ANNA Do you want to play a game, Martin?

MARTIN What game?

ANNA I don't know. You decide.

MARTIN I don't know. I can't think of one.

ANNA How about I think of one that we can both play?

MARTIN Yeah. I don't really want to.

Silence.

ANNA How about arm wrestle? Like you play with Duncan?

MARTIN I do that with Duncan.

ANNA You can do that with me too.

No response.

Martin, you can do that with me too.

MARTIN Oh okay. Nah. Thanks though.

Silence.

Duncan.

No response.

Duncan.

No response.

ANNA Duncan.

MARTIN Duncan…

MARTIN AND ANNA. Duncan.

> *No response.* **MARTIN** *and* **ANNA** *continue to sit in silence.* **DR. RUPERT** *enters. He looks like he is ready to leave for the day. He looks down at* **DUNCAN** *and grimaces for a second and then to* **MARTIN** *and* **ANNA.**

DR. RUPERT Anyone seen Oliver?

MARTIN Toilet.

DR. RUPERT Fair enough. *(A beat)* Home time.

> **DR. RUPERT** *looks down at* **DUNCAN** *once more, grimaces again and exits.*

MARTIN Duncan.

> *No response. Silence.*

ANNA Do you want to know how many brothers or sisters I have?

MARTIN Hmmmh?

ANNA Do you want to know how many brothers and sisters I have, Martin?

MARTIN Okay.

ANNA One brother. One sister.

> *A beat.*

One brother. One sister.

> *A beat.*

MARTIN Huh.

Silence.

Duncan.

No response. **MARTIN** *and* **ANNA** *continue to sit in silence.*

ANNA I am very ticklish.

No response.

I am very ticklish. I love to be tickled. *(A beat)* It's funny but I don't get tickled so much now.

No response.

In Latvia people tickle each other all the time.

Silence.

MARTIN Duncan.

No response. **MARTIN** *and* **ANNA** *continue to sit in silence until* **ANNA** *starts to sing.*

ANNA *(Singing)*

ES IZJĀJU PRŪŠU ZEMI KOKLĒDAMIS, SPĒLĒDAMIS.

*(***DUNCAN** *sits up)*

ANNA *(Singing)*

ES IZJĀJU PRŪŠU ZEMI KOKLĒDAMIS, SPĒLĒDAMIS.

ANNA AND DUNCAN *(Singing)*

PRŪŠU MEITAS MAN' GRIBĒJA PAR JUNKURU
    PATURĒT
PRŪŠU MEITAS MAN' GRIBĒJA PAR JUNKURU
    PATURĒT

ANNA , DUNCAN and MARTIN *(Singing)*
NEPALIKŠU, PRŪŠU MEITAS, MAN PAŠAMI KURZEMĒ,
NEPALIKŠU, PRŪŠU MEITAS, MAN PAŠAMI KURZEMĒ,
MAN PAŠAMI KURZEMĒ᾽ SĒTĀ JAUNA LĪGAVIŅA.
MAN PAŠAMI KURZEMĒ᾽ SĒTĀ JAUNA LĪGAVIŅA.

*(***OLIVER*** enters briskly and angrily. They stop singing. Silence, as* **OLIVER** *glares at the three patients for a couple of seconds.)*

OLIVER Dinner time.

*(***DUNCAN, MARTIN*** *and* **ANNA** *get up and follow* **OLIVER** *to the exit. They smile at each mischievously.)*

Scene Five

NURSE WHITEHALL *and* **ANNA** *are seated together.* **OLIVER** *sits on a chair nearby.*

NURSE WHITEHALL … of course when you're a little girl as I was, then you really think nothing of it. And it wasn't my parents' only umbrella. *(A beat)* Yes, I have a great many memories from Vilnius.

ANNA Vilnius is in Lithuania.

NURSE WHITEHALL Yes, Lithuania.

ANNA I'm from Latvia.

NURSE WHITEHALL Oh, I am silly. I hear Latvia and I think Lithuania because I've been there. Do you find many people do that to you?

ANNA Not really.

NURSE WHITEHALL You like Martin, don't you? I can tell. It takes a woman to tell.

No response.

Oh don't mind Oliver. He knows us girls like to natter. How we like to gossip about such things, don't you, Oliver?

OLIVER *nods.*

He just has to be here in case you attack me.

ANNA I don't want to attack you.

NURSE WHITEHALL I would hope not. But he has to be here. It's a health and safety thing.

Pause.

Men are funny, aren't they? They can drive a woman to distraction. Or somewhere nice on a day trip when things are going well and they want to spend some quality time with you.

NURSE WHITEHALL *laughs.*

ANNA I think men are okay.

NURSE WHITEHALL I think Duncan likes you. Would he be the kind of man you could see yourself settling down with in an alternate reality where neither of you were here?

ANNA I don't like Duncan in that way.

NURSE WHITEHALL Oh well, his loss. *(A beat)* Is there a man back home who writes to you, perhaps? Maybe a tall, handsome man who toils away in Riga, improving himself daily, carrying out maintenance and extension work to his home in the hope that one day you will return and you can live there happy ever after and perhaps start a family?

ANNA No.

NURSE WHITEHALL I've recently had a baby. I'm still not sure what I think or feel about that. She's lovely though. Her name is Charlotte. Everything about her is so small and perfect. Do you have any observations about me and Dr. Rupert?

ANNA How do you mean?

NURSE WHITEHALL Oh how we work together, perhaps. Or how we look standing next to each other? Side-by-side. Perhaps, you've noticed how he looks at me when I'm not noticing? *(A beat)* I mean, does he?

> **ANNA** *shrugs.*

His name is Robert, you know? Robert Rupert. It's like a little poem. My husband is also called Robert.

ANNA Can I go now?

NURSE WHITEHALL Yes.

> **ANNA** *exits. Silence.*

How are you, Oliver?

OLIVER Not bad.

NURSE WHITEHALL Good. I hope you didn't mind me describing men as funny. Trying to get her to open up. Create a bond.

OLIVER We are funny.

NURSE WHITEHALL You are. Oh well. *(A beat)* I should think about lunch. I've only had a piece of toast today.

> **NURSE WHITEHALL** *stands.*

OLIVER He does, you know.

NURSE WHITEHALL Hmmh? What's that?

OLIVER Dr. Rupert. He does look at you when you're not noticing him look at you.

NURSE WHITEHALL Really?

OLIVER All the time.

NURSE WHITEHALL That is odd. I think I'm in love with him. I thought that had gone away, but it hasn't. It's terrible, I'm married to another Robert and have just had a baby. You'd think my heart and mind were there, wouldn't you?

OLIVER We can't help these things.

NURSE WHITEHALL Quite right. You're very unjudgmental. But I don't think that's a word. Isn't that funny?

OLIVER What do you fancy for lunch?

NURSE WHITEHALL Oh, you want to go somewhere?

OLIVER No, thank you. I bring my own lunch.

NURSE WHITEHALL Right. *(A beat)* Okay, so what should I do?

OLIVER About lunch?

NURSE WHITEHALL About Dr. Rupert.

OLIVER Well, what do you want?

NURSE WHITEHALL I don't know. *(A beat)* Well, I want him to like me and do something about it and so then I can decide from there.

OLIVER He won't do anything.

NURSE WHITEHALL Why won't he do anything?

OLIVER You're not really giving him much to go on, are you? And you're married with a baby. And you work together. And he's married too.

NURSE WHITEHALL No, you're right. It is complicated. What do you mean not giving him much to go on?

OLIVER Maybe he needs to know you like him for sure before he does anything.

NURSE WHITEHALL You don't mean tell him?

OLIVER No, don't do that.

NURSE WHITEHALL Thank heavens for that. Perish the thought.

OLIVER Laugh at his jokes, touch him a lot more. Say you're unhappy at home.

NURSE WHITEHALL Really? That sounds brazen.

OLIVER Give him the signals.

NURSE WHITEHALL Signals. Right.

OLIVER You can also be a lot more feminine.

NURSE WHITEHALL I'm not already feminine?

OLIVER You can crank it up a lot more. Dr. Rupert is a high status man. You need to submit to him. It's how these things work. Use your feminine energy.

NURSE WHITEHALL My feminine energy, right.

OLIVER Be more emotional about things.

NURSE WHITEHALL Should I cry in front of him? I mean, I only see him at work. That would be unprofessional.

OLIVER You don't need to cry. Just show more feelings. Less of the matron thing you got going on.

NURSE WHITEHALL Matron thing? Oh dear. And, feelings, well, I'm not sure this is the place for those. Still, I'll give it a bash.

OLIVER You have to make him feel that he wants to protect you.

NURSE WHITEHALL That's fascinating. How do you know all this?

OLIVER I read a lot. I'm also a man.

NURSE WHITEHALL Oh, I'm actually reading a book at the moment too. It's about pirates. I wouldn't recommend it. *(No response)* You've been very helpful.

OLIVER Don't mention it.

NURSE WHITEHALL It flies in the face of everything I've ever known.

OLIVER Play it cool and let the man chase?

NURSE WHITEHALL Precisely.

OLIVER You just end up with a doormat. Not a man as esteemed as Dr. Rupert. He doesn't have the time for all that.

NURSE WHITEHALL Goodness. You're quite right.

OLIVER Let me know how it goes.

NURSE WHITEHALL I expect you'll see for yourself.

OLIVER You go to him. He'll come to you. Just you watch.

NURSE WHITEHALL Thank you, Oliver. *(A beat)* Thank you.

> **NURSE WHITEHALL** *exits. Lights fade.*

Scene Six

Lights up. On a ship at sea, somewhere just off the coast of Latvia. **DR. RUPERT** *enters. He appears relaxed, blissful, happy. Hands on hips, he takes an exaggerated sniff of the air. After a couple of seconds,* **OLIVER** *enters.*

DR. RUPERT Smell that sea air, Oliver. Just smell it.

OLIVER I smell it, Lord Rupert. Very nice. Very, very nice. And please, you don't have to be so formal. Admiral is just fine.

DR. RUPERT Admiral?

OLIVER Yes, Lord Rupert.

DR. RUPERT Right, well, only if you're sure?

OLIVER I'm quite sure, Your Lordship.

DR. RUPERT Admiral it is, then.

OLIVER And where is Her Ladyship?

DR. RUPERT Lady Elizabeth is just freshening up. We've just awoken from a nap. I think I speak for us both when I say that we were absolutely shot earlier.

OLIVER That's understandable. I imagined you would both get tired running up and down the deck, holding hands and laughing and kissing as I saw you do for an hour this morning.

DR. RUPERT Oh you saw that, did you, Admiral?

OLIVER I did Your Lordship. You both looked so…

DR. RUPERT So…?

OLIVER So…

DR. RUPERT So…?

OLIVER So… well, free and happy, Your Lordship.

DR. RUPERT *Free and happy* indeed? Well thank you, Admiral.

    NURSE WHITEHALL *enters.*

DR. RUPERT *(Beaming)* Here she is.

NURSE WHITEHALL *(Glowing)* There you are.

    DR. RUPERT *and* **NURSE WHITEHALL** *embrace warmly and kiss.*

NURSE WHITEHALL Hello, Oliver.

OLIVER Lady Elizabeth. I hope you're feeling rested. And please call me Admiral.

NURSE WHITEHALL Admiral?

OLIVER Yes, Your Ladyship.

NURSE WHITEHALL Very well. Only if you're sure. Hello, Admiral.

DR. RUPERT You know, darling?

NURSE WHITEHALL Yes, darling?

DR. RUPERT The Admiral here made rather an acute observation just now.

NURSE WHITEHALL Did you, Admiral?

DR. RUPERT He did indeed.

NURSE WHITEHALL *(Playfully)* Are you going to tell me what it was or should I guess?

DR. RUPERT *(Laughing gently)* No, I can tell you. *(Stops laughing)* Do you remember this morning when we were running hand in hand and kissing and laughing for at least an hour and maybe more?

NURSE WHITEHALL *(Laughing gently)* Oh yes. I remember.

DR. RUPERT The Admiral was watching us.

NURSE WHITEHALL Were you, Admiral?

OLIVER Yes, Your Ladyship.

DR. RUPERT And he said we looked so free and happy!

NURSE WHITEHALL Oh yes, I suppose we did! What a wonderful and acute observation you made there, Admiral.

OLIVER Well, thank you.

DR. RUPERT Well, how super. Always interesting to receive other people's viewpoints, isn't it?

NURSE WHITEHALL It most certainly is.

Pause.

DR. RUPERT So where are we now, Admiral? I just see sea obviously.

OLIVER We're just off the coast of Latvia, Lord Rupert.

DR. RUPERT Oh how fun.

NURSE WHITEHALL Any icebergs ahead?

OLIVER No, Your Ladyship.

NURSE WHITEHALL Do you get that question a lot?

OLIVER We do.

DR. RUPERT That was dreadful wasn't it? The Titanic.

NURSE WHITEHALL Awful. All those people.

OLIVER It was unfortunate. But no such worries here. The three of us will be just fine.

DR. RUPERT Excellent. Say, I hope you haven't felt like a third wheel on this trip, Admiral.

OLIVER Not in the least, Your Lordship. It is a very big ship for only three people and it does need manning. But thank you for your concern.

> **MARTIN, DUNCAN** *and* **ANNA** *enter, startling* **DR. RUPERT, OLIVER** *and* **NURSE WHITEHALL**. *Perhaps* **NURSE WHITEHALL** *makes a noise of being startled.*

Stay back. Who are you?

ANNA Anna. *(Points to* **MARTIN***)* Martin.

MARTIN Hello.

ANNA *(Pointing to* **DUNCAN***)* Duncan.

DUNCAN Hi there.

OLIVER Where have you come from?

ANNA A boat.

OLIVER I said stay back.

ANNA We mean no harm.

NURSE WHITEHALL Are you pirates?

ANNA No.

DR. RUPERT I see. But you weren't on here when we set sail were you?

ANNA No.

DR. RUPERT And you've just as it were 'got on'.

ANNA Yes.

DR. RUPERT From another boat.

ANNA Yes.

DR. RUPERT So for all intent and purposes you are actually pirates.

ANNA We resist labels.

NURSE WHITEHALL But you're here to steal something presumably?

ANNA No.

DR. RUPERT I see you're the spokeswoman.

MARTIN We don't actually have set roles. But Anna does like to do most of the talking. I make the decisions. I saw this ship in the distance and I said we should probably try to get on it. So here we are. *Voila.*

DR. RUPERT *(To* **DUNCAN***)* And what do you do, er…

A beat.

DUNCAN Oh, Duncan.

DR. RUPERT Sorry, Duncan. Of course. Yes, what do you do, Duncan?

DUNCAN Well, I'm with Anna. In the romantic sense…

NURSE WHITEHALL Oh you're a couple?

ANNA I'm with Martin too.

OLIVER Really?

ANNA Yes.

NURSE WHITEHALL Is this true, Martin?

MARTIN Yes.

DR. RUPERT And how do you feel about that, Duncan?

DUNCAN Well it's not ideal obviously. But Martin's always off having flings with other random women we meet on our travels, aren't you, Martin? That keeps him busy.

MARTIN I can't be tamed. I have a lot of love to give.

DUNCAN So yeah, I do get some time where it's just me and Anna.

ANNA Everyone sort of gets what they want as we adventure together.

MARTIN It's compromise really. *(A beat)* Duncan's a strong swimmer, aren't you, Duncan?

DUNCAN Thanks, mate.

DR. RUPERT Are you?

DUNCAN I have a fish-like love of water.

NURSE WHITEHALL You're quite the trio.

MARTIN Anyway, we're sorry to kind of 'barge on' like this unannounced.

ANNA We were hoping that we could stay.

DUNCAN Yeah. Maybe do some work on the ship. You know, to earn our keep.

OLIVER Now you are talking. Duncan, my friend, you and I are going to be mates.

DR. RUPERT What?

OLIVER I could use the help, your Lordship. It's a really big ship. And I *was* feeling a little bit like a third wheel really.

DR. RUPERT *(With a concern)* Oh Admiral, you should have said.

Silence.

Well, darling?

NURSE WHITEHALL All fine by me. This might all work out rather nicely.

DR. RUPERT Yes. Perhaps it will.

OLIVER Welcome aboard. Let me show you three around. Let's leave these two love birds to it, shall we?

NURSE WHITEHALL AND DR. RUPERT. *(Laughing gently)* Oh, Admiral.

Silence.

NURSE WHITEHALL I know. We should all eat together later!

ANNA That sounds fun.

DUNCAN Yeah, sounds good to me.

DR. RUPERT Bravo! That's settled then. *(A beat)* Welcome aboard!

NURSE WHITEHALL Yes. Welcome aboard!

> **OLIVER, MARTIN, ANNA** *and* **DUNCAN** *exit.*

Gosh.

DR. RUPERT What an unexpected pleasure.

NURSE WHITEHALL Yes.

> **DR. RUPERT** *and* **NURSE WHITEHALL** *smile warmly at each other and kiss. Lights fade.*

Scene Seven

Lights up. Back at the ward. **DR. RUPERT, NURSE
WHITEHALL, MARTIN, DUNCAN** *and* **ANNA** *are seated
together.* **OLIVER** *stands by and watches at a distance
apart from the group.* **DR. RUPERT**, *in particular, seems
a little distracted, out of sorts.*

DUNCAN … and so I just never went back. I just didn't
think people talked like that or did those things
really. It's just a bit fake, isn't it? Also, the seats were
uncomfortable and all the time I was thinking how
much I needed a piss.

DR. RUPERT Okay, good. Let's leave it there, shall we? I
like musicals. Well, I think we're all doing very well.

NURSE WHITEHALL Very well.

MARTIN So are we finishing early today?

DUNCAN Martin.

NURSE WHITEHALL How do you mean, Martin?

DUNCAN Shush, Martin.

MARTIN We still have thirteen minutes.

DUNCAN *(To* **MARTIN***)* Be quiet, will you?

MARTIN Well we do, don't we?

NURSE WHITEHALL *(To* **DR. RUPERT***)* We have run a little
short, Doctor.

DR. RUPERT Is there anything else you want to share? I just
thought everyone looked hungry.

No response.

Well my tummy's rumbling. I'm famished. Ouch.

MARTIN Have you eaten today, Doctor?

DR. RUPERT I haven't, Martin. First day of a new diet. I'm fasting.

NURSE WHITEHALL Oh, Doctor.

DR. RUPERT It's not for much longer. I'm going to grab something for lunch. I don't really know how people manage it.

NURSE WHITEHALL You should always eat.

DR. RUPERT I really should. *(A beat)* But yes okay, we can go the whole hour if you want to.

DUNCAN No, it's okay. We're fine.

ANNA Cleaning jobs.

DUNCAN Yeah, jobs for us around here. Let's talk about that.

> **DR. RUPERT** *looks to* **NURSE WHITEHALL**.

NURSE WHITEHALL Not right now, Duncan. What else?

Silence.

MARTIN How about the elephant in the room? Let's talk about that.

> **DR. RUPERT** *looks to* **NURSE WHITEHALL** *again.*

NURSE WHITEHALL Do you mean suicide, Martin? Do you feel like that? Do any of you feel like that?

MARTIN No, the elephant in the room. I don't know, I just hear people say that. I just wonder if we have one. An elephant.

Silence.

DUNCAN He doesn't mean anything. He's just saying things.

DR. RUPERT Yes, I got that, Duncan.

Pause.

MARTIN I don't know… why are we here?

NURSE WHITEHALL Why are you here?

MARTIN Why are we here?

DR. RUPERT Why are *you* here?

MARTIN No. Why are *we* here? On earth, I mean.

DR. RUPERT That's a big question, Martin.

MARTIN Thanks.

Pause.

DUNCAN We can talk about work around here. For us. Let's do that.

A beat.

DR. RUPERT Why *are we* here, Martin? Okay, woof. I wish I had the answers. I mean, yes, who are we, really? At the end of the day? Who are you?

MARTIN *(Under his breath)* Martin.

DR. RUPERT *(Ignoring* **MARTIN***)* …or who am I?

MARTIN *(Under his breath)* Dr. Rupert.

NURSE WHITEHALL Martin.

MARTIN Sorry.

DR. RUPERT …what *are we*? What is anything really? Look at the animal kingdom. I mean, good lord. Then there's God of course. Or look at the cosmos, if you believe in that kind of thing. What are we in the grand scheme? We are but little things. Is that Shakespeare? Sounds like something he would say. Write.

NURSE WHITEHALL I'm not sure.

DR. RUPERT No.

NURSE WHITEHALL It sounds nice anyway. "We are but little things".

DR. RUPERT Yes. We're molecules really. With hopes and with dreams. Some of us are athletes and musicians and world leaders. Some have greatness thrust upon them. That is Shakespeare. I think I just made up the other thing. *(A beat)* Yes, some of us are kings and queens, generals, scientists… and some among us are tramps of course. With our hands out and an over rehearsed hard luck story. We all have a tale, don't we? A story. A serious history. Who knows, Martin? I hope I've gone some way in answering your question. Look to the ancients. It goes back to the Greeks probably. *(A beat)* I've been there of course. Athens.

NURSE WHITEHALL Have you, Doctor?

DR. RUPERT Athens? Yes. Uhm, we went for our honeymoon. Elizabeth and I.

NURSE WHITEHALL Oh… how lovely.

DR. RUPERT It was alright. But it was during a heat wave.

MARTIN Very hot, then?

DR. RUPERT It was very hot, Martin. Never known anything like it. That first afternoon we climbed up to the Acropolis. We brought the camera. Took some pictures. And that was it really. We spent the rest of the week in bed. We were young and foolish, we'd contracted sunstroke, we hadn't worn hats or applied sunscreen. Yes, buggered the whole holiday just on that first day really.

NURSE WHITEHALL How awful.

DR. RUPERT Yes, on the one hand, Nurse Whitehall, it was truly awful. On the other hand, I don't know, it was rather… I don't know, nice. It sort of brought us together. Curtains drawn, we pined for England and lower body temperatures and we dabbed each other

with cold, wet cloths. Through the fever, the diarrhea
and the vomiting, we even laughed about it a little.
If you can imagine that. But that was then obviously.
(A beat) I'm sounding wistful. I think it's my hunger
pains. I'm beginning to think I'll go with a soup and a
sandwich for lunch. I'm ravenous.

NURSE WHITEHALL They illuminate the Acropolis when
the sun goes down, don't they? I've seen the brochures.
It's very pretty.

DR. RUPERT They do indeed.

DUNCAN You probably should have gone up then. At that
time, I mean. You might have had more of a holiday.

DR. RUPERT Well, perhaps, Duncan. Perhaps.

Silence.

DUNCAN So what about the work?

MARTIN Yes. What about the cleaning?

DR. RUPERT Oh, for Heaven's sake.

ANNA Just let us do something!

Pause.

DOCTOR. Nurse?

NURSE. Yes, Doctor?

DOCTOR. One moment?

NURSE. Yes, Doctor.

> **NURSE** *and* **DOCTOR** *move to an area away from the
> earshot of* **DUNCAN**, **ANNA** *and* **MARTIN**. *They confer
> quietly between themselves. While this goes on* **OLIVER**
> *pulls out his mobile phone and sneaks a look at it.*

OLIVER *(Holds up his phone)* Margaret Thatcher's died!
Stroke. *(Puts back his phone)* Fuck. Sorry.

DR. RUPERT Really? How?

MARTIN A stroke. Oliver said.

DR. RUPERT And I was just telling you all about the time I had sunstroke.

NURSE WHITEHALL A stroke? Goodness.

DR. RUPERT A stroke. Well, that'll do it sometimes. One of those, I mean. Oh how sad.

MARTIN Oh no. You knew her didn't you, Oliver?

NURSE WHITEHALL Did you, Oliver?

ANNA He Skyped with her.

NURSE WHITEHALL *Did you?*

MARTIN While he was in the Shetlands.

NURSE WHITEHALL Oh, well that sounds like a story I would like to hear some time, Oliver.

DR. RUPERT Yes, Oliver, you dark horse. *(A beat)* Well, gosh. RIP. That's really knocked me for six. I thought she'd go forever. Just goes to show I was way off with that one. *(A beat)* End of an era really.

NURSE WHITEHALL Or the beginning of a new one.

DR. RUPERT True. We're also in the middle of some ongoing eras right now too of course. Does anyone have the right words for something like this? I'd be surprised quite honestly.

NURSE WHITEHALL Yes, sometimes silence is better.

DR. RUPERT Good idea.

MARTIN Silence is golden. That's a song.

DR. RUPERT Very good, Martin.

DUNCAN What about our jobs?

DR. RUPERT Please, Duncan. Have some respect. We're in mourning.

ANNA I feel okay.

MARTIN Me too.

DUNCAN I want a job around here.

DR. RUPERT Yes, yes, Duncan. Let's just remember The Iron Lady for two ticks and we'll get to that later.

MARTIN Let's have a minute of silence.

DR. RUPERT Oh good idea.

MARTIN I've never done one for anybody. I always think I'd laugh.

DR. RUPERT No, they'll be none of that. If we're going to do one, we're going to do it properly.

NURSE WHITEHALL Quite right, Doctor.

DR. RUPERT Glad you agree, Nurse. Okay, on your marks, get set, go.

A brief silence. **MARTIN** *bursts out laughing.*

NURSE WHITEHALL Martin!

MARTIN I'm sorry, Nurse Whitehall.

DR. RUPERT Okay, that was a practice. We had a couple of seconds there. Let's try next time to go the whole hog.

Pause.

Are we ready? Annnnndddd silence…

A slightly lengthier silence. **MARTIN** *affectedly puts his hand on his heart.*

DUNCAN We're not singing the national anthem, Martin.

DR. RUPERT Duncan!

NURSE WHITEHALL Oh, Duncan. We were doing well there.

DR. RUPERT *(Impatiently)* Okay, how's this? No minute of silence for Lady Thatcher and no chance for any little jobs we may be able to give you on the ward.

Silence.

Good. And a one and a two and a one, two, three, four.

About twenty seconds of silence as all stand frozen. **OLIVER** *stands giving a military salute. And then…*

Is anyone counting?

Scene Eight

DR. RUPERT *and* **MARTIN** *are seated together.* **OLIVER** *sits on a chair nearby.*

DR. RUPERT … and I suppose looking back, she was only in it for the fun really. And when we stopped having fun, she said 'Sayonara'.

MARTIN Was she Japanese?

DR. RUPERT No. She was from Bristol actually.

Silence.

MARTIN Still, you met your wife later? That's a good thing.

DR. RUPERT Yes, true.

MARTIN You don't seem happy about that.

DR. RUPERT Don't I? Oh well, I suppose I miss her, Martin.

MARTIN Where is she?

DR. RUPERT She'll be at home now in our house. *(A beat)* But I miss what she used to be like. Since this whole 'trying' thing began. So much strain. Every time we hug now it's one of commiseration, not joy. When we have… when we make love it's just to reproduce and in the back of your mind you know that it's just going to lead to post mortem and self loath every month... It's so… I don't know. I don't know what it is.

MARTIN You feel lonely?

DR. RUPERT Well, it's not for a psychiatrist to say, Martin but a little.

MARTIN Well I hope you get your baby.

DR. RUPERT So do I, Martin. So do I. Strange how everything you've worked for seems so pointless when you can't get something like that right. It seems so basic.

MARTIN I don't think I want children.

DR. RUPERT Ah, you say that now, but one day you could well wake up and think won't it be wonderful having something real to love and invest in. To watch grow, and be a better person than you ever could. A new smile, a new laugh and a new person in your life to love and to love you. It's marvelous. It's a miracle. *(A beat)* Of course, lots to do for you Martin before you can start thinking like that. You'd need to pass an evaluation to get out of here first. Or alternatively have your parents sign your release.

> **NURSE WHITEHALL** *enters.*

Nurse Whitehall?

NURSE WHITEHALL I'm sorry, Doctor. Is this a bad time? Hello, Martin.

DR. RUPERT A little. Can it wait?

NURSE WHITEHALL I've seen a spider.

DR. RUPERT Oh. Right. That's not nice.

NURSE WHITEHALL I don't like them. I need protecting. Ha!

DR. RUPERT Ha! Is Gavin not around somewhere?

NURSE WHITEHALL *(A little disappointed)* Yes, he is.

DR. RUPERT Maybe he can help you?

> *Pause.*

NURSE WHITEHALL Yes, Doctor.

> **NURSE WHITEHALL** *exits.*

DR. RUPERT Sorry about that, Martin. *(A beat)* Don't really know what all that was about.

MARTIN A spider. I don't really like spiders either.

DR. RUPERT No? Oliver, how do you feel about them?

OLIVER Don't mind them.

DR. RUPERT Me neither. That was very odd. What's funny is I've seen her handle a spider on the summer staff picnic and there wasn't as near a fuss as that. Still, she's fantastic, isn't she?

MARTIN Who's that?

DR. RUPERT Nurse Whitehall.

MARTIN Who's to say?

DR. RUPERT Well me, Martin. Between us three, I wish we'd have had an affair and then just saw where it went.

MARTIN Blimey.

DR. RUPERT She has the same name as my wife, you know. I'm not sure whether that would have made things easier to navigate or not.

MARTIN Who's to say?

DR. RUPERT Indeed. Does she look happy to you?

MARTIN Who's to say?

DR. RUPERT Please stop saying that, Martin.

MARTIN Sorry, Doctor.

DR. RUPERT Anyway, let's wrap up with something about you, Martin. How are you expressing yourself daily?

MARTIN I don't know what you mean.

DR. RUPERT Are you still drawing?

MARTIN I can't draw.

DR. RUPERT Oh nonsense. Your pictures were lovely. Weren't they, Oliver? I hope you haven't given up.

OLIVER That was George.

DR. RUPERT George of course. Sorry, Martin. It was George. Still, it would be a shame not to take a stab at it yourself. It made George very happy drawing away before he escaped from here in the middle of the night. You never met George, did you?

MARTIN What happened to George?

DR. RUPERT Oh he ran away and couldn't be found.

MARTIN How did you find out?

DR. RUPERT He left us a note, Martin.

MARTIN What did it say?

DR. RUPERT "I've ran away and I can't be found."

MARTIN Wow. Just like that.

DR. RUPERT Yes, and he was right. We couldn't find him. It's not an episode that we take a lot of pride in really. There was quite a black cloud hanging over this place until we forgot about it and all moved on.

MARTIN Can I go now?

DR. RUPERT Oh what's the rush? Let's do something boysy.

MARTIN Doctor?

DR. RUPERT I'm joking. Ha! Thank you, Martin.

MARTIN *exits.*

We have our work cut out there, I think.

Silence. **DR**. **RUPERT** *gathers his things.*

OLIVER She doesn't look happy.

DR. RUPERT Who doesn't look happy?

OLIVER Nurse Whitehall. You asked if she looked happy. She doesn't look happy. Not to me anyway.

DR. RUPERT Is that right? You've noticed that too. Do you think it's a post-natal depression of some kind? But you thought she would have mentioned it. I think I'm in love with her. I hope you can keep a secret.

OLIVER What's that?

DR. RUPERT I just told you. I think I'm in love with her.

OLIVER Oh.

DR. RUPERT How do I go about this, Oliver? You're a young man of the world. *(A beat)* How do you tell someone you're in love with that you like them like that? In that very big and magical way? And of course I'm married that's the thing. That's the turd in the party punch.

OLIVER She's married too. And she's just had a baby.

DR. RUPERT You're right. The timing's rotten. And I don't even know if she likes me. I don't know, do you see any signs of that?

OLIVER Not really.

DR. RUPERT Dammit.

OLIVER But that doesn't mean anything.

DR. RUPERT It doesn't?

OLIVER You just need to activate it.

DR. RUPERT *Activate it?* Activate what?

OLIVER Her attraction for you.

DR. RUPERT Oh, so she'll have some lurking for me somewhere, then? Potentially? That's promising. And so how do I go about that, then?

OLIVER Pure masculine energy.

DR. RUPERT Masculine energy?

OLIVER Yeah. Do you have any?

DR. RUPERT Well, I'm not quite sure what it is. Should I smash something up in front of her?

OLIVER How are you when you're with her?

DR. RUPERT Oh I panic, mostly. I mean, I'm potty about her and it just feels so wrong. But when I calm down I'm very accommodating towards her.

OLIVER See that has to go. You need to be strong, masculine, aloof and focus on your purpose.

DR. RUPERT Which is?

OLIVER You're a doctor.

DR. RUPERT I know I am. But I don't know what my purpose is. That's what I'm asking you.

OLIVER That's your purpose. You're a doctor.

DR. RUPERT Oh, I see.

OLIVER You're a doctor. She's a nurse. Maintain that distance. It'll drive her crazy for you.

DR. RUPERT Like be unattainable, you mean?

OLIVER Exactly. It's like catnip for women. It's a challenge.

DR. RUPERT Really? But won't she just give up?

OLIVER They never give up.

DR. RUPERT Interesting. So I can't talk to her? I would really miss that actually. And I work with her.

OLIVER You can. But just respond to anything she says like a high status man. No emotions in reaction to anything she says.

DR. RUPERT No emotions? Well, it's all very British this, I must say. And it sort of makes sense and sounds kind of fun. I like it, Oliver. I'll give it a whirl.

DUNCAN *enters.*

Hello, Duncan.

DUNCAN Doctor.

DR. RUPERT *(To* OLIVER*)* Are we finished here? I think I've got the picture.

OLIVER Good luck.

DR. RUPERT *considers for a moment and then hugs* OLIVER *and then exits. Silence.*

DUNCAN Where's Anna?

OLIVER Don't know.

Silence.

Sings.
"SPLISH, SPLASH. I WAS TAKING A BATH"

DUNCAN Don't mind baths.

OLIVER *(Sings)*
"SPLISH SPLASH!"

DUNCAN Don't mind. I like 'em.

OLIVER Pussy.

DUNCAN Dick.

DUNCAN *starts to exit.*

OLIVER Hey, listen, Dunconi. *(A beat)* Duncan.

> **DUNCAN** *stops and turns around.*

DUNCAN What?

OLIVER Come here.

DUNCAN What?

OLIVER Just come here. Come and sit down for a moment. Come on.

> **DUNCAN** *tentatively follows* **OLIVER** *and they both take a seat. Brief silence.*

DUNCAN What?

> *Pause.*

OLIVER I don't like this tension between you and me.

DUNCAN Tension?

OLIVER Yeah, I feel there's a tension between us.

DUNCAN Well, you pick on me, don't you?

OLIVER *(Considers for a moment)* Yeah.

> *Silence.*

DUNCAN Is that it?

> **DUNCAN** *gets up.*

OLIVER No, no. Sit back down a sec.

> **DUNCAN** *sits back down.*

I'd like to help you out.

DUNCAN What with?

OLIVER The Anna situation.

DUNCAN Anna?

OLIVER The Latvian. *(A beat)* You like her, eh Dunc?

Silence.

She likes you. You like her. It's a situation and I want to help you.

DUNCAN I don't think she likes me.

OLIVER It's not what she told me, mate.

DUNCAN What did she tell you?

OLIVER That she likes you.

DUNCAN I think she likes Martin. Not me.

OLIVER Why do you think that?

DUNCAN She follows him everywhere and she avoids me.

OLIVER Ah, women do that, mate. When they like you. They go off with another bloke and avoid you so you wonder about them. So you want them more. It's the oldest trick in their book.

DUNCAN Really?

OLIVER You can take that to the bank.

DUNCAN She told you she likes me?

OLIVER She's nuts about you, mate.

DUNCAN I don't know.

OLIVER Martin's like her alibi.

DUNCAN A decoy, you mean.

OLIVER Yeah, that's what I meant. Not an alibi. Martin's a decoy. It's probably to make you jealous.

DUNCAN It's working. I feel awful.

OLIVER Well you need to step up and be the man in this situation and go and get her. You need to lead. You're too passive. You've got to be like… James Bond.

DUNCAN James Bond?

OLIVER Or any of those guys in the films. The ones who get the birds. They don't just do nothing, do they?

DUNCAN I don't do nothing.

OLIVER Come on, mate. I've seen you. The three of you are sitting around. Her and Martin are just chilling out and talking or what have you and you're just sitting in the corner or you lay face down on the floor. It sends out the wrong message, mate. You're playing it too cool.

DUNCAN You think? *(A beat)* But I do ask her to do things with me and she always –

OLIVER It's beating about the bush is what that is, Dunc. Tell her how you feel. Women love that. Lay it all out for her. What you have planned for both of you going forward. They love all that. Certainty, planning.

DUNCAN I don't know. *(A beat)* It's being here.

OLIVER Well you can mention all that.

DUNCAN About being here?

OLIVER Yeah.

DUNCAN What about it?

OLIVER What you were going to say.

Silence.

Look. Just be honest about your feelings. About your emotions.

DUNCAN You really think so?

OLIVER They go in big for all that stuff. And she's not going to know otherwise and you may lose her for good.

DUNCAN Really?

OLIVER She's aching for you to do that. Trust me.

Silence.

DUNCAN Okay. *(A beat)* Okay. I'll do it.

OLIVER Good man.

DUNCAN Yeah. *(A beat)* Yeah.

OLIVER I just couldn't stand by any longer and not do anything.

DUNCAN *smiles at* **OLIVER**.

DUNCAN Well, thanks. I owe you one.

OLIVER Ah, you're welcome.

DUNCAN No. I mean it. *(A beat)* You're all right.

DUNCAN *puts out his hand to shake and* **OLIVER** *takes it.* **DUNCAN** *gets up to exit.*

I just need to think it through. Plan what I'm going to say. I want to get it just right.

OLIVER Of course. But I mean it, don't wait too long.

DUNCAN I won't. *(A beat)* Thank you. *(A beat)* Mate.

OLIVER *nods.* **DUNCAN** *exits.*

Scene Nine

DR. RUPERT *is eating a McDonalds meal and staring straight ahead, chewing.* **NURSE WHITEHALL** *enters. They remain at a distance apart.*

NURSE WHITEHALL Doctor.

No response.

Doctor?

DR. RUPERT Nurse.

NURSE WHITEHALL You were in a world of your own.

DR. RUPERT Oh just mulling things over. Making masculine decisions. How are you?

NURSE WHITEHALL I'm feeling emotional. I suppose that's very feminine of me. I've just been watching television.

DR. RUPERT Anything good?

NURSE WHITEHALL Just that ghastly news about that soldier.

DR. RUPERT Oh? Which soldier? I haven't heard.

NURSE WHITEHALL A soldier's been killed.

DR. RUPERT Really? Oh well that happens a bit.

NURSE WHITEHALL It was two men that did it.

DR. RUPERT Ah, a duo.

NURSE WHITEHALL It was a machete attack.

DR. RUPERT A machete attack?

NURSE WHITEHALL Islamic fundamentalists, they say.

DR. RUPERT At it again, eh?

NURSE WHITEHALL It was very barbaric.

DR. RUPERT They can be barbaric. It's crackpot doolally over there.

NURSE WHITEHALL This was in Woolwich.

DR. RUPERT Woolwich?

NURSE WHITEHALL It was outside some army barracks. They hit him with a car.

DR. RUPERT Gosh.

NURSE WHITEHALL Then they attacked him with knives and a meat cleaver. Dragged his body into the middle

of the road and left him there. Then they spoke for a bit to the cameras. Well, one of them did. The other just sort of stood around awkwardly.

DR. RUPERT He spoke for a bit to the cameras? This was televised? What did he say?

NURSE WHITEHALL Something about revenge for what happens in their land or something. He had blood on his hands.

DR. RUPERT It sounds like he does.

NURSE WHITEHALL No, you could see for yourself. He had blood on his hands. You'll have to watch it later.

DR. RUPERT I expect I might.

NURSE WHITEHALL Then the police arrived and shot them both.

DR. RUPERT Oh so a somewhat happy ending.

NURSE WHITEHALL It was all so terrible. I actually got quite upset.

DR. RUPERT Oh well. There, there.

NURSE WHITEHALL You think of the family in times like this.

DR. RUPERT You think of everything in times like this. My friend Gordon owns residential properties in Woolwich.

NURSE WHITEHALL Well, I hope he will be safe.

DR. RUPERT Oh no, he lives in Chelsea. I was just thinking of house prices etc. That's his game. Property. *(A beat)* But that's the unemotional response to this, perhaps.

Silence.

NURSE WHITEHALL I thought you would understand.

DR. RUPERT Understand what, Nurse?

Pause.

NURSE WHITEHALL Never mind. *(A beat)* I should probably go and do something. I'll leave you to your lunch, Doctor.

DR. RUPERT Good idea, Nurse.

Silence. **NURSE WHITEHALL** *begins to exit and stops.*

NURSE WHITEHALL You've been acting strangely recently. Is everything okay?

DR. RUPERT Have I? I really hadn't noticed.

NURSE WHITEHALL *begins to exit.*

You've been acting rather strangely yourself.

NURSE WHITEHALL Really? I don't think so.

Silence.

DR. RUPERT Don't go.

NURSE WHITEHALL Sorry?

DR. RUPERT I mean, well we should probably talk.

NURSE WHITEHALL *(Expectantly)* Oh?

DR. RUPERT Uhm, yes.

NURSE WHITEHALL About what?

Silence.

Doctor?

DR. RUPERT Yes. This erm, the erm... the... cleaning business. The work thing they keep harping on about.

NURSE WHITEHALL Oh. Yes?

DR. RUPERT I'll call a meeting. Just follow my lead.

NURSE WHITEHALL Is that it?

DR. RUPERT Yes.

NURSE WHITEHALL Okay.

DR. RUPERT And... ahm, how's Charlotte?

NURSE WHITEHALL She's doing well, thank you.

DR. RUPERT Do you still have those pictures on your phone?

NURSE WHITEHALL Yes. *(A beat)* Do you want to see?

DR. RUPERT Do I?

NURSE WHITEHALL Do you?

DR. RUPERT I don't know. Do you want me to?

NURSE WHITEHALL Do I?

DR. RUPERT Do you?

NURSE WHITEHALL AND DR. RUPERT. Probably should.

A beat.

DR. RUPERT I'd like to see a picture of your daughter.

NURSE WHITEHALL Of course.

She takes out her phone and passes it **DR. RUPERT**. *Brief silence.*

DR. RUPERT She's lovely. You three look so happy.

A beat.

NURSE WHITEHALL Thank you.

Pause.

DR. RUPERT I knew I'd lose you in the end.

A beat.

NURSE WHITEHALL I knew I'd lose you in the end.

Pause.

DR. RUPERT We never really had each other at all really. Not at any point.

NURSE WHITEHALL No.

DR. RUPERT It just seemed like something nice and sad to say. Just then.

NURSE WHITEHALL Yes. And it was. It was nice. And it was sad.

DR. RUPERT Yes. *(A beat)* Sad about that soldier too.

NURSE WHITEHALL Yes.

> **NURSE WHITEHALL** *exits.*

Scene Ten

> **NURSE WHITEHALL** *and* **ANNA** *are seated together.*

NURSE WHITEHALL What are men afraid of, Anna?

ANNA I don't know.

NURSE WHITEHALL I mean, you just have to look at the news to see that they do so many incredible things. They invest in things and they invent cures for things and they make all kinds of money. All those sports they play and think of all the kinds of medals and trophies and knighthoods they win.

ANNA Yes.

NURSE WHITEHALL All those clever things they say and do, and the wonderful sarcastic comments they make. And the books they write, the pictures they paint, the music they make and just think of all those photographs they've taken.

ANNA It's a mystery.

NURSE WHITEHALL Then there's the killing and raping, and the invading and bombing of countries, and the pillaging. When they set out to do something they often do it. Men can really get things done. But they just can't express their true feelings in any reasonable way. Just what are they afraid of? Just what do they think we would do?

ANNA shrugs. DUNCAN enters.

DUNCAN Hello, Anna.

ANNA Hello, Duncan.

NURSE WHITEHALL Hello, Duncan.

DUNCAN Hi. Where is everybody?

NURSE WHITEHALL They should be here soon.

DUNCAN Can I speak to Anna for a second? In private.

NURSE WHITEHALL I don't think so, Duncan.

DUNCAN Anna?

NURSE WHITEHALL If it's about the cleaning, Dr. Rupert and are going to talk to you all about that very shortly.

DUNCAN It's not about that.

NURSE WHITEHALL Well, I think if you have anything to say, I think you can say it front of me too.

DUNCAN Okay. So Anna. Maybe it's always been there, I don't know, but I've sensed a distance between us. Like when I ask you to do something with me, you don't really want to do it. When I look for you, I can never find you and when I try to talk to you, you ignore me. I suppose what I'm trying to say is, I just want to know where we stand.

No response.

NURSE WHITEHALL Duncan.

DUNCAN I sometimes ask myself whether this is really the right environment for us, you know? I mean, there's here and there's the common area and that's pretty much it. There's our rooms, but we're not allowed in each other's rooms and I don't think the corridor is conducive for, well, you name it.

ANNA Duncan.

DUNCAN I've known pain. Anyone I've ever shown kindness or fondness of, they've just kind of ran away. And on some occasions even left the country. I don't know, I guess I just stopped doing that for a while. I got cynical. I got scrappy. Spent too much time on my own. But it's not who I truly was and somehow I've wound up in here. But I want to change and I want to go back. I want to go back to how I used to be and love with abandon. And I want you.

ANNA Duncan, I don't like you like that.

DUNCAN Okay. Thanks for letting me know.

> **DUNCAN** *takes a seat. A silence. Finally,* **DR. RUPERT** *enters followed by* **OLIVER** *and* **MARTIN**. **MARTIN** *takes a seat.* **NURSE WHITEHALL** *gets up and stands by* **DR. RUPERT**. **OLIVER** *remains standing and finds a spot a distance apart from the group.*

DR. RUPERT Friends, Latvians and Countrymen! Lend me your ears. Ha. *(A beat)* No seriously, listen up and to why we've called you here. You see Nurse Whitehall and I have had a good old chat. We personally think we do a bang up job of keeping the place ship shape and spic and span. But we're not of made of stone and if one of you wants to go round with a mop and bucket and feel better about it and clean what the cleaners have already cleaned, just to feel like you're doing something, well we could probably accommodate that. And as it was Anna's idea, we've decided she should be the one allowed to do it.

NURSE WHITEHALL I will show you where everything is, Anna.

DR. RUPERT Knock yourself out, as they say, Anna. Congratulations, Anna.

> **DR. RUPERT** *and* **NURSE WHITEHALL** *applaud and* **MARTIN** *joins in.*

DUNCAN *Anna*???!! Instead of one of us? She's from Latvia!

NURSE WHITEHALL Oh dear.

DUNCAN If anything it should be me or Martin. What happened to looking after your own? This is England. In-ger-land! Who cares if it was her idea??!

NURSE WHITEHALL Duncan.

MARTIN Why can't we all do a little each?

DUNCAN Oh grow some balls, will you, Martin! Do you not see what's happening here?

> *Silence.*

This is… SHIT!

DR. RUPERT *(To* **OLIVER***)* Oliver ? Can you show Duncan back to his room?

DUNCAN Oh come on. You're having us on!

> **OLIVER** *nods. And starts to herd* **DUNCAN** *off stage. He takes* **DUNCAN** *by the arm.* **DUNCAN** *resists.*

Don't touch me!

> **OLIVER** *much bigger than* **DUNCAN** *grabs* **DUNCAN** *tighter.*

Okay, I'm going. I'm going!

> **OLIVER** *and* **DUNCAN** *exit. Noises of their struggle continue off stage.*

DR. RUPERT Well, quite. (*To* **ANNA** *and* **MARTIN**) So?

ANNA I don't want to be the only one who gets to do something.

MARTIN Can we not both do it, Doctor? Me and Anna.

NURSE WHITEHALL We've already told you, Martin. No.

ANNA You can do it, Martin. If you want to. You do it.

MARTIN I don't want to, if you can't.

ANNA One of us should. You do it.

> *A sound of a shower turned on and sounds of screaming and shouting from a distressed* **DUNCAN** *can be heard off stage through the following.*

DR. RUPERT I think we should let Martin have the final say.

MARTIN (*Becoming agitated*) No I don't want to have the final say. No I don't.

DR. RUPERT Let's make Martin make the important final decision.

NURSE WHITEHALL Yes, come on, Martin.

MARTIN (*Increasingly agitated*) No I don't want to make the important final decision. I don't.

DR. RUPERT Five seconds, Martin.

MARTIN (*Very agitated*) What? You're confusing me.

NURSE WHITEHALL FIVE…

DR. RUPERT Nothing confusing here, Martin. Either you get to and Anna doesn't. Or she gets to and you don't.

NURSE WHITEHALL FOUR…

DR. RUPERT Running out of time, Martin. Quick decision needed.

MARTIN (*Remarkably agitated to* **ANNA**) What should I say??!!

NURSE WHITEHALL THREE…

ANNA Leave him alone. I'll do it. I'll do it!

NURSE WHITEHALL TWO…

MARTIN Please…

ANNA Leave him alone!

NURSE WHITEHALL ONE…

The off stage noises from **DUNCAN** *stop.*

MARTIN I… I don't…

DR. RUPERT And we're out of time. Sorry, Martin. *(A beat)* Hard luck, Anna.

MARTIN I… I'm sorry, Anna.

ANNA It's okay, Martin… it's okay…

> **OLIVER** *re-enters he is soaking wet. He nods to* **DR. RUPERT**.

DR. RUPERT Phew. That was all a storm in a teacup. *(A beat)* Now I really must get going. I will see you all on Thursday.

> **MARTIN** *nods.* **ANNA** *nods reluctantly.*

Good. Nurse Whitehall.

NURSE WHITEHALL Good luck with your golf, Doctor.

DR. RUPERT Thank you, Nurse. Enjoy your afternoon, won't you?

> **DR. RUPERT** *exits.*

NURSE WHITEHALL When you're both ready, I think you should join the rest of us in the common area. Read the newspapers. Watch the television. It's what it's there for. Mmmh?

NURSE WHITEHALL *exits. Followed by* **OLIVER**. *A silence, and then.*

ANNA I love you, Martin.

A beat.

MARTIN Thanks.

Silence.

MARTIN We'll be all right here, won't we, Anna?

Pause.

ANNA Yes, Martin. *(A beat)* If we stick together…

ANNA *puts out her hand.* **MARTIN** *tentatively takes it. A brief silence.*

MARTIN I'm thirsty.

Lights fade on **ANNA** *and* **MARTIN**.

End of Play

Property Plot

Set: Psychiatric ward in England (p1)
Packed lunch (p9)
Chairs – a few as in a hospital ward (p9)
Oliver's mobile phone (p9)
Handbag (p15)
Apples x2 (p15)
Chair (p26)
Set: Ship at sea off the coast of Latvia - (Author's Note: this is optional to have the ship), or just an indication of the ship(p31)
Set: Back in the psychiatric ward (p38)
Chairs x5 (p38)
Chairs x3 (p45)
Dr. Rupert - gathers his things (p49)
McDonalds meal (p55)
Nurse Whitehall's mobile phone (p59)
Chairs x2 (p60)
Oliver is soaking wet (p65)

Sound Effects Plot

Noises of a struggle between Oliver and Duncan (p63)
A sound of a shower turned on and sounds of screaming and shouting from a distressed Duncan can be heard off stage (p64)
The off stage noises from Duncan stop (p65)

Lighting Plot

Lights fade (p31)
Lights up (p31)
Lights fade (p37)
Lights up (p38)
Lights fade (p66)